POSTCARD POEMS

Edited by Paul B. Janeczko : :

POSTCARD POEMS

A Collection of Poetry for Sharing

Bradbury Press   Scarsdale, New York

Library of Congress Cataloging in Publication Data
Main entry under title:
Postcard poems.
Summary: A collection of 100 brief poems by such poets as William Carlos Williams, Richard Brautigan, Langston Hughes, Ezra Pound, Cid Corman and Carl Sandburg.
    1. American poetry—20th century.   2. Children's poetry, American. [1. American poetry— Collections]
I. Janeczko, Paul B.
PS613.P67   811'.5'08   79-14192
ISBN 0-87888-155-7

Grateful acknowledgment is made for permission to use copyrighted material.

"Gift" by Judith Hemschemeyer: Copyright © 1973 by Judith Hemschemeyer. Reprinted from I REMEMBER THE ROOM WAS FILLED WITH LIGHT, by permission of Wesleyan University Press.

"Poeti-c Art" by Arudra: Reprinted by permission of the Asian Studies Center, Michigan State University.

"The Poem" by William Carlos Williams: From COLLECTED LATER POEMS by William Carlos Williams. Copyright © 1944, 1948 by William Carlos Williams. Reprinted by permission of New Directions.

"Some Uses of Poetry" by Eve Merriam: Reprinted by permission of Atheneum Publishers from IT DOESN'T ALWAYS HAVE TO RHYME by Eve Merriam. Copyright © 1964 by Eve Merriam.

"Things Men Have Made" by D. H. Lawrence: From THE COMPLETE POEMS OF D. H. LAWRENCE, edited by Vivian de Sola Pinto and F. Warren Roberts. Copyright © 1964, 1971 by Angelo Ravagli and C. M. Weekley, Executors of The Estate of Frieda Lawrence Ravagli. All rights reserved. Reprinted by permission of Viking Penguin, Inc., Laurence Pollinger Limited, and the Estate of the late Mrs. Frieda Lawrence.

"The Beautiful Lawn Sprinkler" by Howard Nemerov: From THE COLLECTED POEMS OF HOWARD NEMEROV, University of Chicago Press, 1977. Reprinted by permission of the author.

"Scrap Iron" by Raymond Durgnat: © Raymond Durgnat. Reprinted by permission of the author.

"A Trucker" by Thom Gunn: Copyright ©

Sharing is a celebration. You know the feeling. You feel it every time you give a gift to someone: a smile trying to break out of you when you give your friend a handful of wildflowers—maybe sea lavender or swamp candles that you've picked along the side of the road or at the edge of the salt marsh. Maybe you've felt the celebration when you found a tiny shell or a stone worn smooth by the sea and knew exactly the person you were going to give it to. Whenever you give to someone, you know the celebration of sharing.

The poems in this collection are gifts from the poets, meant to be shared. Each poem is a sharing of a vision that is unique to each poet. Some of the poems are sad, some are joyous. Others are angry or tender. In the opening poem, "Gift," Judith Hemschemeyer offers to "wrap a poem around you." You may not like the feel of all of the poems here, but that's all right because poets don't necessarily seek to make you feel comfortable. Others may feel comfortable at first reading, like an old coat worn smooth by the hungry hands of winter. You may linger over others, return to them every time you open the book. But do allow each poet the chance to "wrap a poem around you." Let each poet share her or his vision of experience.

I hope that the poems in this collection touch you. But don't let them rest after they've made their impression. Let them touch someone else. When you find one that delights you, jot it down on a postcard, or on a notecard, or even at the end of a letter. Each of the 104 poems here is brief enough for jotting, hence the title, *Postcard Poems*.

Good poetry is an endangered species. It needs to be protected from extinction. It needs to be nurtured by people who delight in it. Share these poems with a friend who needs to know he's not alone. Or with someone who needs to smile. Or with the person who revels in the power of words. If you like the poems, pass them on!

Paul B. Janeczko
Auburn, Maine

With love, this collection is for Mark
—friend, brother, and White Sox fan.

Contents : :

Let me wrap a poem around you—
Not now, when the curve of your life,
Like a mile-wide Pacific wave
Is rising, rushing you along,
Tons of sweet water supporting every limb—

But sometime, if ever you are thrown down
On some strange beach, or hurt, or so in love
With someone that you dare not make a start.
Then let me approach and offer you these words,
A poor shawl for your perfect throat.

Arudra (Bhagavatula Sankara Sastri) ::
<u>Poeti–c Art</u>
(*translated by B.V.L. Narayana Row*)

The poetic cart
has two wheels
equal
and efficient

what to say
and how

neither
is superior
to the other

if either one
is missing
there is
no cart
moving

2

It's all in
the sound. A song.
Seldom a song. It should

be a song—made of
particulars, wasps,
a gentian—something
immediate, open

scissors, a lady's
eyes—waking
centrifugal, centripetal

to paint without a palette
to dance without music
to speak without speaking

to feel the strangeness between hot and cold
to feel the likeness of hot and cold
to plunge into both at the same moment

Things men have made with wakened hands, and put soft life into
are awake through years with transferred touch, and go on glowing
for long years.
And for this reason, some old things are lovely
warm still with the life of forgotten men who made them.

5

What gives it power makes it change its mind
At each extreme, and lean its rising rain
Down low, first one and then the other way;
In which exchange humility and pride
Reverse, forgive, arise, and die again,
Wherefore it holds at both ends of the day
The rainbow in its scattering grains of spray.

Raymond Durgnat ::
Scrap Iron

A black steel carcass in a field of sheep
Repels the drench of light and weeps out rust
Lamenting gulped-up roads, the hedgerows smeared and blurred,
The bucking bridges and the startled birds.

The slow sap struggles to the screaming sun,
The lark upspirals on her simple song;
My spring is broken and my winter long,
This cold steel slowly burns to be a gun.

7

Sometimes it is like a beast
barely controlled by a man.
But the cabin is lofty
as a skull, and all the rest
extends from his foot as an
enormous throbbing body:

if he left anything to
chance—see his great frame capsize,
and his rubber limbs explode
whirling! and see there follow
a bright fountain of red eyes
tinkling sightless to the road.

Cars are wicked, poets think.
Wrong as usual. Cars are part of man.
Cars are biological.
A man without a car is like a clam without a shell.
Granted, machinery is hell,
But carless man is careless and defenseless.
Ford is skin of present animal.
Automobile is shell.
You get yourself a shell or else.

9

This strange thing must have crept
Right out of hell.
It resembles a bird's foot
Worn around the cannibal's neck.

As you hold it in your hand,
As you stab with it into a piece of meat,
It is possible to imagine the rest of the bird:
Its head which like your fist
Is large, bald, beakless and blind.

It goes fwunkety,
   then shlunkety,
as the washing goes around

The water spluncheses
   and it shluncheses,
as the washing goes around.

As you pick it out it splocheses,
   then it flocheses,
as the washing goes around.

But at the end it schlopperies,
   and then flopperies,
and the washing stops going round.

The birds—are they worth remembering?
Is flight a wonder and one wingtip a
space marvel?
When will man know what birds know?

A silver jet,
riding the top of tundra clouds,
comes over
maybe from Rio:
the aluminum sun shines
on it
as if it were a natural creature.

the butterfly it's
              a crazy toy
mechanical and
              wound up it goes
like a pub-crawler
              to the open throats of flowers.

The butterfly, a cabbage-white,
(His honest idiocy of flight)
Will never now, it is too late,
Master the art of flying straight,
Yet has—who knows so well as I?—
A just sense of how not to fly:
He lurches here and here by guess
And God and hope and hopelessness.
Even the aerobatic swift
Has not his flying-crooked gift.

William Heyen ::
The Snapper

He is the pond's old father, its brain
and dark, permanent presence.

He is the snapper, and smells
rich and sick as a mat of weeds; and wears

a beard of leeches that suck frog, fish,
and snake blood from his neck; and drags

a tail ridged as though hacked out
with an ax. He rises: mud swirls

and blooms, lilies bob, water washes
his moss-humped back where, buried

deep in his sweet flesh, the pond ebbs
and flows its sure, slow heart.

I love crows.
If I met one human size
I'd invite him into my living room
and offer him the softest chair.
Then we'd crack a fifth of Old Human
and talk late into the night.
The room would be filled
with the shine and rustle of his feathers
and the wit of his sharp eye.

I saw the two starlings
coming in toward the wires.
But at the last,
just before alighting, they

turned in the air together
and landed backwards!
that's what got me—to
face into the wind's teeth.

Visible, invisible,
    a fluctuating charm
an amber-tinctured amethyst
    in habits it, your arm
approaches and it opens
    and it closes; you had meant
to catch it and it quivers;
    you abandon your intent.

IV

If flowers want to grow
right out of the concrete sidewalk cracks
I'm going to bend down to smell them.

Not even dried-up leaves,
skidding like ice boats on
their points down winter streets
can scratch the surface of
a child's summer and its wealth:
a stagnant calm that seemed
as if it must go on and on
outside of cyclical variety
the way, as child-height on a wall,
a brick named "Ann"
by someone's piece of chalk
still loves the one named "Al"
although the street is vacant and
the writer and the named are gone.

No David could send a stone as high
As one of these buildings, most birds fly
Above them or avoid the city entirely,
Even sparrows who need little prosperity
Sense how many of their number are seized
Dipped in peroxide and sold for canaries
By small Puerto Rican boys, who send me to hell,
And fly into battle with broken aeriels.

22

It is a squad car idling
through my eyes, bored,
looking for a crime to crush.
Two tough cops drive in,
three years on the same beat,
sick of each other.
To it I am no better
than a radish.
I hear its indolent engine
grump along in second gear,
feel both cops watch me
walk with stiff ankles,
a nun among drunks.

The pawn-shop man knows hunger,
And how far hunger has eaten the heart
Of one who comes with an old keepsake.
Here are wedding rings, and baby bracelets,
Scarf pins and shoe buckles, jeweled garters,
Old-fashioned knives with inlaid handles,
Watches of old gold and silver,
Old coins worn with finger marks.
They tell stories.

On Watching the Construction of a Skyscraper

Nothing sings from these orange trees,
Rindless steel as smooth as sapling skin,
Except a crane's brief wheeze
And all the muffled, clanking din
Of rivets nosing in like bees.

The confines of a city block
Cut to a monument, exact,
At all points rectilinear,
From air a perfect square intact,

As trim as Plato thought or Eu-
Clid drew with stick. What thinker put
This idea into cubes to sell
At fifty cents a cubic foot?

O neat, O dead, what feeling thing
Could buy so bare! O dead, O neat,
What beating heart could sink to buy
The copy of the die complete!

About an excavation
a flock of bright red lanterns
has settled.

27

V

When despair for the world grows in me
and I wake in the night at the least sound
in fear of what my life and my children's lives may be,
I go and lie down where the wood drake
rests in his beauty on the water, and the great heron feeds.
I come into the peace of wild things
who do not tax their lives with forethought
of grief. I come into the presence of still water.
And I feel above me the day-blind stars
waiting with their light. For a time
I rest in the grace of the world, and am free.

Quick!

Empty the offices
rush all the lecture halls
abandon the copy machines
burst out

EMERGEN—

see the sky
unboxed
lid off
shaking loose

What number do we call to
bring it down
box it
back in?

It's a late starting dawn that breathes my vision,
inhales and exhales the sound of waking birds
And pokes ten miles of cold gray sky at a deer
    standing alone in a meadow.

The sky of gray is eaten in six places,
Rag holes stand out.
It is an army blanket and the sleeper
    slept too near the fire.

31

on the rock overlapping the huddled rock-gorge
on the rock planted on rock for a wall
on the rock rusted with a rosy haze in it
on the rock children scrawl with chalk
   as though that were a way of making it talk
you can see circling about with a crazy velocity
as if the grain of the rock were reassembling
   for some unforeseeable purpose
red specks that are the tiniest spiders
          if you look real close

Not slowly wrought, nor treasured for their form
In heaven, but by the blind self of the storm
Spun off, each driven individual
Perfected in the moment of his fall.

Dawn breaking as I woke,
With the white sweat of the dew
On the green, new grass
I walked in the cold, quiet as
If it were the world beginning;
Peeling and eating a chilled tangerine.
I may have many sorrows,
Dawn is not one of them

Where the dusty lane
Wound dull and plain
Among blind weeds,
Today daisies
Have opened a petal-
Decorated way
For us to walk;
The two fluttering, white-
Fringed, golden-eyed banks
Seem wide celebrations—
As if earth were glad
To see us passing here.

Sounds like big
rashers of bacon frying.
I look up from where I'm lying
expecting to see stripes

red and white. My eyes drop shut,
stunned by the sun.
Now the foam is flame, the long
troughs charcoal, but

still it chuckles and sizzles, it
burns and burns, it never gets done.
The sea is
fat.

Birds are flowers flying
and flowers perched birds.

A perfect rainbow! a wide
arc low in the northern sky
spans the black lake

troubled by little waves
over which the sun
south of the city shines in

coldly from the bare hill
supine to the wind which
cannot waken anything

but drives the smoke from
a few lean chimneys streaming
violently southward

VI

Our car was fierce enough;
no one could tell we were only ourselves;
so we drove, equals of the car,
and ate at a drive-in where Citizens were dining.
A waitress with eyes made up to be Eyes
brought food spiced by the neon light.

Watching, we saw the manager greet people—
hollow on the outside, some kind of solid veneer.
When we got back on the road we welcomed
it as a fierce thing welcomes the cold.
Some people you meet are so dull
that you always remember their names.

*(Newspaper "personal" items: Sadie,
the cleaning woman, please call Mrs. Blake.)*

Sadie
the cleaning lady:
"I ain't stud'n her
cause I dun got
tired from my nose
to my toes of
Miz Blake (alias Miz Ann)
messing aroun' to make
one month's dirt be a day!!"

So bandit-eyed, so undovelike a bird
to be my pastoral father's favorite—
skulker and blusterer
whose every arrival is a raid.

Love made the bird no gentler
nor him who loved less gentle.
Still, still the wild blue feather
brings my mild father.

41

To clothe the fiery thought
In simple words succeeds,
For still the draft of genius is
To mask a King in weeds.

Occasional mornings when an early fog
Not yet dispersed stands in every yard
And drips and undiscloses, she is severely
Put to the task of herself.

Usually here we have view window dawns,
The whole East Bay at least some spaces into the room,
Puffing the curtains, and then she is out
In the submetropolitan stir.

But when the fog at the glass pauses and closes
She is put to ponder
A life-line, how it chooses to run obscurely
In her hand, before her.

She stands
In the quiet darkness,
This troubled woman
Bowed by
Weariness and pain
Like an
Autumn flower
In the frozen rain,
Like a
Wind-blown autumn flower
That never lifts its head
Again.

Just so you shouldn't have to ask again,
He was the kind of guy that if he said
Something and you were the kind of guy that said
You can say that again, he'd say it again.

I watched a man in a cafe fold a slice of bread
as if he were folding a birth certificate or looking
at the photograph of a dead lover.

Karl Szelki ::

The chestnut vendor
must shout to be heard above
the October wind.

That hump of a man bunching chrysanthemums
Or pinching-back asters, or planting azaleas,
Tamping and stamping dirt into pots,—
How he could flick and pick
Rotten leaves or yellow petals,
Or scoop out a weed close to flourishing roots,
Or make the dust buzz with a light spray,
Or drown a bug in one spit of tobacco juice,
Or fan life into wilted sweet-peas with his hat,
Or stand all night watering roses, his feet blue in rubber boots.

So is the child slow stooping beside him
picking radishes from the soil.
He straightens up,
his arms full of the green leaves.
She bends low to each bunch and whispers,
Please come out big and red.
Tugs at them gently to give them time to change,
if they are moody and small.
Her arms filled, she paces
beside her grandfather's elderly puppet walk.

VII

The child is on my shoulders.
In the prairie moonlight the child's legs
    hang over my shoulders.
She sits on my neck and I hear her calling
    me a good horse.
She slides down—and into the moon silver of
    a prairie stream.
She throws a stone and laughs at the clug-clug.

Through jaggedy cliffs of snow, along sidewalks of glass,
Footing unsure, as on a fun-house floor,
A little girl goes, all dressed in black, a Prince
Hamlet himself. In black velvet dress
(under her coat), black stockings (really tights)
And patent leather pumps, solemn white face,
And finally white frill blouse and a gold locket
As finishing touch, she makes her way,
Bearing an enormous pink and tinfoil box
Tied with a bow of deeper pink.

The box reflects its blush along the high snow walls
As the little prince slips hurriedly up the path
And turns three doors away like a live toy
Into the castle of the birthday party.

He'd found some lumber from an old fence rotting
By the woods, and raised it up,
And said it was a fort that he was making,
But the blue jay, knowing better, cried out, "Thief!"
Because the urgent hammer, fast and fierce,
Was nailing the October day to woodsmoke and
The birches and the wind;
Now it was his to keep—the boy's and not the jay's,
His day for good and all, and so
The outraged bird cried "Thief!" and flew
To find his own day in some other place.
The boy worked as the wind blew colder and the day grew long;
It was his fort, he said, and he would make it strong.

Paul Zimmer ::
Zimmer's Head Thudding Against the Blackboard

At the blackboard I had missed
Five number problems in a row,
And was about to foul a sixth,
When the old, exasperated nun
Began to pound my head against
My six mistakes. When I cried,
She threw me back into my seat,
Where I hid my head and swore
That very day I'd be a poet,
And curse her yellow teeth with this.

Two girls of twelve or so at a table
in the Automat, smiling at each other
and the world; eating sedately.
And a tramp, wearing two or three tattered coats,
dark with dirt, mumbling, sat down beside them—
Miss Muffit's spider.
But, unlike her, they were not frightened away,
and did not shudder as they might if older and look askance.
They did steal a glance
at their dark companion and were slightly amused:
in their shining innocence seeing
in him only another human being.

Robert Graves ::
The Hero

Slowly with bleeding nose and aching wrists
After tremendous use of feet and fists
He rises from the dusty schoolroom floor
And limps for solace to the girl next door
Boasting of kicks and punches, cheers and noise,
And far worse damage done to bigger boys.

55

A young Apollo, golden–haired,
    Stands dreaming on the verge of strife,
Magnificently unprepared
    For the long littleness of life.

I went to school
With the biggest pusher
This side of the Mississippi.
Of course he wasn't
When we were in school.
(If he was, I didn't know.)

He was just one of the gang,
A smiling face amongst others,
Smiling now from a
Yellowed
Yearbook page.

Friends said: about eight o'clock they used to come
and call us to our windows, at eight, when light
was still enough to see by. Nice girls, but some
were lonely, and would come up and stay the night,

they said. And others said, by the Starnberger See
the waitresses swimming beneath the pier
would giggle and call up to us and play
hide and seek with us and murmur, wir sind hier,

so those friends said. And in the crowded night
girls gone or gray are calling to my friends
who now are gray or gone, to share the light
of lost long days before midsummer ends.

In tight pants, tight skirts,
stretched or squeezed,
youth hurts.
Crammed in, bursting out,
Flesh will sing
And hide its doubt
In nervous hips, hopping glance,
Usurping rouge,
Provoking stance.

Put off, or put on,
Youth hurts. And then
It's gone.

59

VIII

When you are in love, we love the grass,
And the barns, and the lightpoles,
And the small main streets abandoned all night.

What do we need for love—a midnight fire
Flinging itself by fistfuls up the chimney
In soft bright snatches? Do we need the snow,
Gentle as silence, covering the scars
Of weeks of hunger, years of shabby having?
Summer or winter? A heaven of stars? A room?
The smiling mouth, the sadness of desire
Are everywhere the same. If lovers go
Along an unknown road, they find no less
What is familiar. Let them stay at home,
And all will still be strange. This they know
Who with each heartbeat fight the fear of change.

Love which is the most difficult mystery
Asking from every young one answers
And most from those most eager and most beautiful—
Love is a bird in a fist:
To hold it hides it, to look at it lets it go.
It will twist loose if you lift so much as a finger.
It will stay if you cover it—stay but unknown and invisible.
Either you keep it forever with fist closed
Or let it fling
Singing in fervor of sun and in song vanish.
There is no answer other to this mystery.

Your smile,
with the spectacular softness
of a rainbow,
makes me
laugh and wish I were
the sky.

63

Chipmunks jump, and
Greensnakes slither.
Rather burst than
Not be with her.

Bluebirds fight, but
Bears are stronger.
We've got fifty
Years or longer.

Hoptoads hop, but
Hogs are fatter.
Nothing else but
Us can matter.

I had long known the diverse tastes of the wood,
Each leaf, each bark, rank earth from every hollow;
Knew the smells of bird's breath and of bat's wing;
Yet sight I lacked; until you stole upon me,
Touching my eyelids with light finger-tips.
The trees blazed out, their colors whirled together,
Nor ever before had I been aware of the sky.

IX

The Old Men Admiring Themselves in the Water

I heard the old, old men say,
"Everything alters,
And one by one we drop away."
They had hands like claws, and their knees
Were twisted like the old thorn-trees
By the waters.
I heard the old, old men say,
"All that's beautiful drifts away
Like the waters."

And the days are not full enough
And the nights are not full enough
And life slips by like a field mouse
                   Not shaking the grass.

Once I was jealous of lovers. Now I am
jealous of things that outlast us—the road
between Route 28 and our house, the bridge
over the river, a valley of second-growth trees.
Under the birches,
vines, the color of wolves, survive a winter
ten below, while the unpicked apples turn black
and the picked fruit is red in the basket.
I am not sure that the hand of God
and the hand of man ever touched, even by chance.

They are not long, the weeping and the laughing,
    Love and desire and hate:
I think they have no portion in us after
    We pass the gate.

They are not long, the days of wine and roses:
    Out of a misty dream
Our path emerges for a while, then closes
    Within a dream.

I have nothing new to ask of you,
Future, heaven of the poor.
I am still wearing the same things.

I am still begging the same question
By the same light,
Eating the same stone,

And the hands of the clock still knock without entering.

X

It's already autumn, and I've suffered other months
without learning anything
except that I lost you
for too much love like a hungry man
overturning the bowl
with his trembling hands.

71

In the shut drawer, even now, they rave and grieve—
To be approached at times with the frightened tear;
Their cold to be drawn away from, as one, at nightfall,
Draws the cloak closer against the cold of the marsh.

There, there, the thugs of the heart did murder.
There, still in murderer's guise, two stand embraced, embalmed.

Music, when soft voices die,
Vibrates in the memory—
Odors, when sweet violets sicken,
Live within the sense they quicken.
Rose leaves, when the rose is dead,
Are heaped for the beloved's bed;
And so thy thoughts, when thou are gone.
Love itself shall slumber on.

73

Wang Chung-ju ::
Complaint of a Young Girl
(*translated by Kenneth Rexroth*)

Nobody but me can know the sorrow that wrings me.
Weeping I return to my obscurity
I keep from the past only bitterness
In the present there is only black emptiness.

I send you back your gifts, jewels, earrings,
The fur jacket I wore in the old days,
You can tie up a broken string
But never put back together a broken heart.

74

When dreams like stars collide,
some race through space
and scatter themselves in perfect
array through the night.
Others fall like fiery snow,
covering everything:
your heart,
our love,
and finally my face.

He had done for her all that a man could,
And, some might say, more than a man should.
Then was ever a flame so recklessly blown out
Or a last goodbye so negligent as this?
"I will write to you," she muttered briefly,
Tilting her cheek for a polite kiss;
Then walked away, nor ever turned about . . .

Long letters written and mailed in her own head—
There are no mails in a city of the dead.

XI

Your absence has gone through me
Like thread through a needle.
Everything I do is stitched with its color.

With a sadness curtained
Windows
   Left behind

She steps along a beach
Abandoned now

And with a stick left by a
Wave
   Protesting still

Upon sands she knows must
Wander

Scrawls her name.

Coming home on a summer night
To the empty house—it's like being
On colorless TV, on the stage set
For Return of the Grand Insomniac;
It is to watch your life as it would be
Without you: the old druggist in the darkroom
Developing someone else's negatives.

Others because you did not keep
That deep-sworn vow have been friends of mine;
Yet always when I look death in the face,
When I clamber to the heights of sleep,
Or when I grow excited with wine,
Suddenly I meet your face.

All night I wore the phone, a dead scarf,
charred bone of a bishop's mistress.
There was a drone, as if a distant lawn
were being mown.
And I was dying, dying upwards
like pines in a dense grove.
And all I had were these words;
put them down a slot
and they ring like flattened bells,
discs of doused fire.
Come home, come home,
my lungs are thick with the smoke of your absence.

As if I carried a charm
for daughters, I would carve a smile
each day and enter it, see it
between us like a pumpkin glowing.
    Out of its hollow mouth,
    the candle burned away.

No one will smooth her now
with promises. But when the sun comes
through the glass, I see her face,
smell the milky wrinkle of her skin,
    feel the small shape of light
    going out of my arms.

The World Is Not a Pleasant Place to Be

the world is not a pleasant place
to be without
someone to hold and be held by

a river would stop
its flow if only
a stream were there
to receive it

an ocean would never laugh
if clouds weren't there
to kiss her tears

the world is not
a pleasant place to be without
someone

XII

They sit on the wall at the square

From the steps behind
coming up from below
you can see the row of their backs

black buckles dangling
from dusty black vests

James Russell Lowell ::
Sixty-Eighth Birthday

As life runs on, the road grows strange
With faces new, and near the end
The milestones into headstones change,
'Neath every one a friend.

85

The last time I kissed her
I held a thin sparrow
her bones were that hollow.

Where did she get the juice to turn
her eyes, to laugh at her great grandson
singing her jingle bells?

Now for my little dry wren
a cardboard box could serve as nest.
Too frail for feathers, she took my kisses,

waving come back, come back again.

86

P. *Wolny* ::
Harmonica Man
(for *my grandfather and Robbie*)

In a one-button gray wool sweater
and lopsided corduroy bedroom slippers,
the ancient, wifeless, shrunken man
wheezes warm beer-breath
through the slots of his gold harmonica.
The family applauds his polkas, but
sad, cataracted eyes
look through nearly ninety years
at the rock in the brook smooth face
of his great-grandson
as the four year old claps and shouts for more.
The old man smiles,
begins another song,
perhaps hoping if he keeps on playing
he can keep from dying.

The left side of her world is gone—
the rest sustained by memory
and a realization: There are still the children.

Going down our porch steps her pastor
calls back: "We are proud of her recovery,
and there is a chiropractor up on Galesburg . . ."

The birthdays of the old require such candles.

His tundra'd mind sprouts leaflets
here and there
and causes me to stare
in new awareness of the man
he must have been.
Where he now
         struggles
              to retain
such meagre lichen to his brain
he must have raised
rare orchids
years ago.

When you are old and gray and full of sleep,
And nodding by the fire, take down this book,
And slowly read, and dream of the soft look
Your eyes had once, and of their shadows deep;

How many loved your moments of glad grace,
And loved your beauty with love false or true
But one loved the pilgrim soul in you,
And loved the sorrows of your changing face.

And bending down beside the glowing bars
Murmur, a little sadly, how love fled
And paced upon the mountains overhead
And hid his face amid a crowd of stars.

90

XIII

Walt Whitman ::
Memories

How sweet the silent backward tracings!
The wanderings as in dreams—the meditation of old times
    resumed—their loves, joys, persons, voyages.

91

How did it come ungathered, all the sheaved throng
of graces and good-byes? Dandelion-blown in the strong
wind, time's spindrift-whirling pressure, our young

moment of together and yesterday flies
the storm. The date enacts and dies.
How can I hold the look in your eyes?

How pull and store thistledown out of the blast?
It slipped, air-caught, at the last.
Sweet wind, sweet wind, where have you blown our past?

This cannon cannot shoot again; but sits, a relic in the park,
And coke cans conquer cannon balls stuffed down the silent
    muzzle. Think;
Shells replaced by soft drink tins, the Civil War subdued by
    soda.
This cannon fired at Perryville and saw six thousand men go
    down—
Kentucky freed as Buell sang a charge that singed the gray
    dust blue.
The town square succeeds battle fields, trimmed grass surrounds
    a bloodless ground.
Once photographed by Brady, now it's Kodaked by the Lions Club,
Sticky children scale a barrel burnished by artillerymen;
Mute history stands on wooden wheels and aims at Woolworth's
    Five and Ten.

Old men stand
Leaning lazily against
A tired old fence.
Faded eyes follow a bulldozer
Tearing down the house
Years ago a palace in their eyes.

Minds wandering see
Parties on the lawn,
Beauties on the porch,
First loves walking by,
All never yielding
To a bulldozer approaching.

Last night I dreamed of an old lover,
I had not seen him in forty years.
When I awoke,
I saw him on the street:
his hair was white,
his back stooped.
How could I say hello?
He would have been puzzled all day
about who the young girl was
who smiled at him.
So I let him go on his way.

it comes back
unopened

why open
to see what I said

there was
much to tell you

now there is nothing
to say

Here lies wrapped up tight in sod
Henry Harkins c/o God.
On the day of Resurrection
May be opened for inspection.

97

Then, when the child was gone,
I was alone
In the house, suddenly grown huge.
   Each noise
Explained itself away
As bird, or creaking board, or mouse,
Element or animal.
But mostly there was quiet as after
   battle
Where round the room still lay
The soldiers and the paintbox and the
   toys.
But when I went to tidy these away,
I felt my mind swerve:
My body was the house,
And everything he'd touched, an ex-
   posed nerve.

P. Wolny ::

Words, Like Spiders

(for Max Watson, d. 4/1/79)

The caved-in cardboard box
squats at the end of the closet,
unseen by all except
my cat, who sometimes sleeps on it,
and me, who never looks at it.
Your words are hiding inside—
small, thread-legged spiders
dancing across a paper web
that took three years to spin—
ready to crawl through the darkness
and wake me with their screams.

99

Richard Snyder ::

A Small Elegy

(for "Cougar" Crissinger
which name she gave herself)

Ann Eleanor, a child of ten,
her joy her only regimen,
shinnied a firedrake maple tree
and fell into eternity,
into a child forever ten,
her flaming joy at apogee.
The maple's leaves burned bright and then
followed her bright vivacity.

There is not a poem in sight,
only my father running out
upstairs, and me without a nickel
for the meter. The children hide
before the television
shivering in its glacial light,
and shivering I rub these words
together, hoping for a spark.

Surely a dead moth's
the skull of a tiny horse,
and the moon's a saint
who pities the sea.

Peace, peace to this child
of rain and light,
and the people who stay
holding candles and lilies,

tasting their tears,
naked in a dream,
over the long drawer
they've closed in the earth.

Death is great.
We are his
with laughing mouth.
When we think ourselves in the midst of life,
he dares to weep
in the midst of us.

103

No labor-saving machine,
Nor discovery have I made,
Nor will I be able to leave behind me any wealthy
    bequest to found a hospital or library,
Nor reminiscence of any deed of courage for America,
Nor literary success, nor intellect, nor book for the
    book-shelf,
But a few carols vibrating through the air I leave,
For comrades and lovers.

Index of Poets : :